Pit Vipers

Adam G. Klein
ABDO Publishing Company

visit us at
www.abdopub.com

Published by ABDO Publishing Company, 4940 Viking Drive, Edina, Minnesota 55435.
Copyright © 2006 by Abdo Consulting Group, Inc. International copyrights reserved in all
countries. No part of this book may be reproduced in any form without written permission from
the publisher. The Checkerboard Library™ is a trademark and logo of ABDO Publishing
Company.

Printed in the United States.

Cover Photo: Peter Arnold
Interior Photos: Corbis pp. 5, 6, 7, 8, 9, 11, 12, 15, 17, 18, 19, 21

Series Coordinator: Megan Murphy
Editors: Heidi M. Dahmes, Megan Murphy
Art Direction & Maps: Neil Klinepier

Library of Congress Cataloging-in-Publication Data

Klein, Adam G., 1976-
    Pit vipers / Adam G. Klein.
        p. cm. -- (Snakes. Set II)
    ISBN 1-59679-282-5
    1. Pit vipers--Juvenile literature. I. Title.

QL666.O69K55 2005
597.96'3--dc22
                                                                                          2005047828

CONTENTS

PIT VIPERS

There are about 200 species of **venomous** snakes known as vipers. Vipers have a pair of long, hollow fangs that are attached to movable bones in their jaws. These fangs can be folded back when not in use.

The viper **family** is divided into two subfamilies, Viperinae and Crotalinae. The Crotalinae group consists of pit vipers. These snakes have a heat-sensing pit on each side of their head. Common pit vipers include rattlesnakes, water moccasins, and copperheads.

The largest group of pit vipers is rattlesnakes. There are about 30 species of rattlesnakes throughout North and South America. Pit vipers without rattles are mostly found in tropical areas. These snakes include the Malayan pit viper and the bushmaster.

Snakes are reptiles, which are vertebrates. This means they have a backbone, just like humans. All reptiles have scales as skin. They shed their skin several times a year.

Snakes are cold-blooded. This means they rely on an outside heat source to maintain their body temperature. So, pit vipers can often be seen sunning themselves during the day. They hunt primarily at night when it is cooler.

Venom drips from the hollow, folding fangs of this prairie rattlesnake. The fangs of some pit viper species can be 1.4 inches (4 cm) long!

SIZES

Pit vipers come in various sizes. The average pit viper is between three and five feet (1 and 2 m) long. The bushmaster is the largest of all the pit vipers. This snake can reach lengths of 11 or 12 feet (3 or 4 m). But, the smallest pit vipers are less than two feet (.5 m) in length.

The bushmaster's scientific name is Lachesis muta. This is Latin for "silent fate." Compared to other pit vipers, the bushmaster produces enormous amounts of venom.

Pit vipers are generally stouter snakes. However, **arboreal** species are often more slender than **terrestrial** species. Pit vipers are best identified by their broad, lance-shaped head. And, all pit vipers have **vertical** pupils.

Rattlesnakes vary in size. The pygmy rattlesnake is less than 18 inches (46 cm) long. However, this eastern diamondback may become eight feet (2 m) long.

Pit vipers also have a row of single scales reaching across the underside of their bodies near the tail. Most other snakes have a double row of scales in this area.

COLORS

Pit vipers across the world come in all different colors. They can be bright green, yellow, brown, or gray. Some pit vipers are marked with patterns of different colored scales. However, a pit viper's color is usually not enough to identify it properly.

Rattlesnakes are most easily identified by the rattle at the end of their tail. These snakes are usually gray or light brown in color. But some can be orange, pink, red, or green.

Because of its coloring, this sidewinder rattlesnake is able to hide on the desert floor.

They often have dark diamonds, **hexagons**, or spots on a lighter background.

This green tree viper is found primarily in Asia. It lives in forest and grassland regions. But sometimes, it appears in towns and cities!

WHERE THEY LIVE

Pit vipers live in all kinds of **habitats**. Some live in jungles. Others live in deserts. Pit vipers also live in mountains and forested hills. Some rattlesnakes, as well as the water moccasin, live in wetland areas. The bushmaster lives in **humid** forests, usually near rivers.

Pit vipers are generally **terrestrial**, although some species are **arboreal**. The water moccasin is actually semi-**aquatic**. Most pit vipers only come out in the evening and night hours.

In the winter, some pit viper species gather in dens to hibernate. They find a safe place underground where they are protected from the cold. They spend the entire winter in a sleeplike state. When the outside temperature gets warmer, they become active again.

The copperhead is the most common pit viper found in the eastern United States.

WHERE THEY ARE FOUND

There are hundreds of types of pit vipers spread throughout the world. These snakes can be found in North and South America, as well as southeastern Europe. Pit vipers also live all across Asia, including India, Japan, and Malaysia.

The Sumatran pit viper is a member of the group of Asian lance-headed pit vipers. This snake is found in Malaysia.

Rattlesnakes are found from Canada to South America. They usually occupy hot, dry regions. Water moccasins and copperheads are found in the eastern to southeastern part of the United States.

The two largest species of pit vipers live in Central and South America. The fer-de-lance is found from the coast of Mexico to northern Argentina. The bushmaster's **habitat** extends from Costa Rica to Brazil.

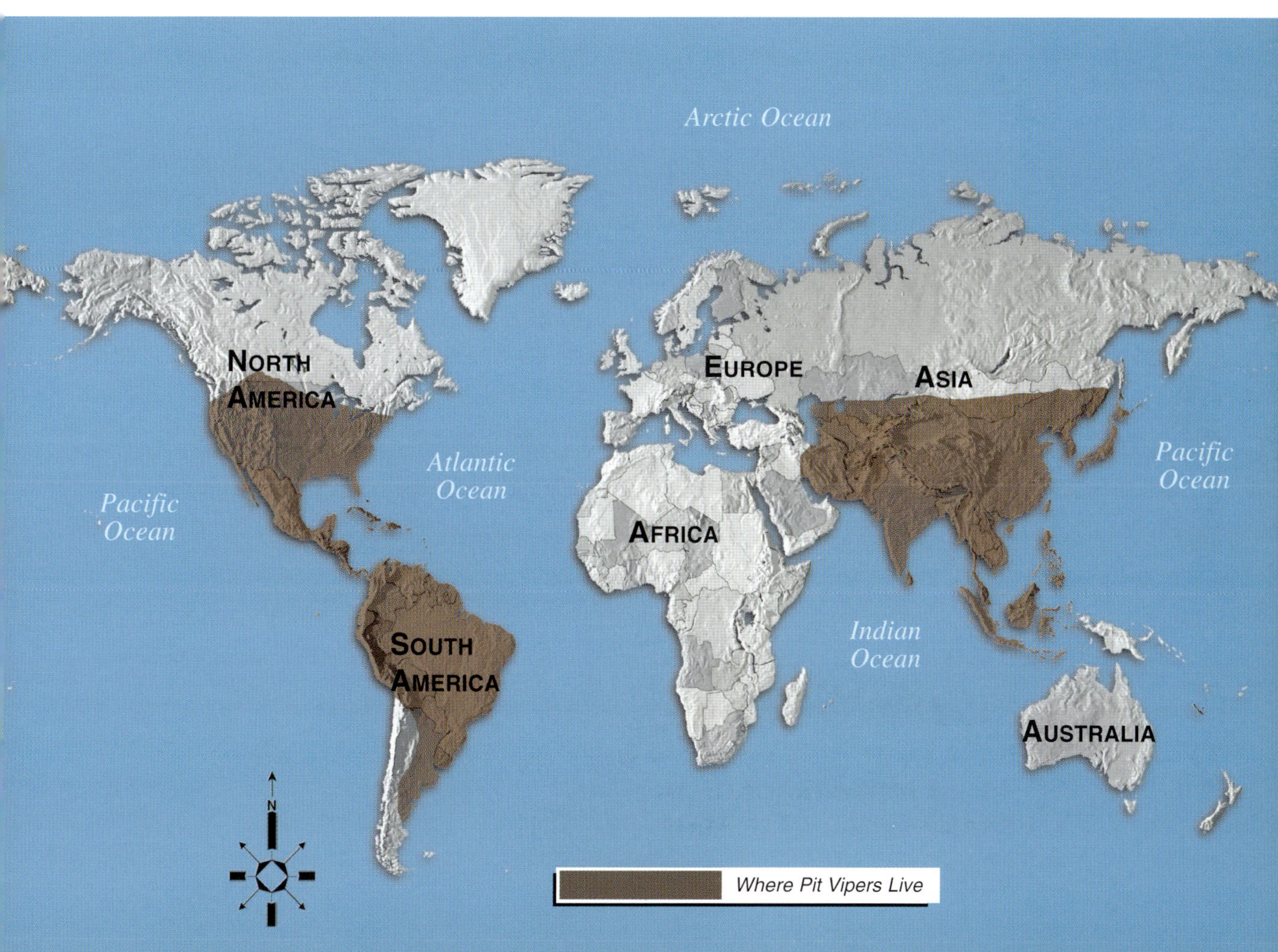

SENSES

The pit viper's name comes from the two heat-sensing pits on its head. A pit sits between the eye and nostril on each side of its head. With these pits, the snake can sense heat given off by a creature's body.

The pits are lined with a layer of cells that contain **thermoreceptors** connected to the snake's brain. These thermoreceptors help pit vipers determine small changes in temperature. They can detect changes as small as 0.002 degrees Fahrenheit (0.001°C).

Pit vipers use the information from their heat-sensing pits to locate prey or avoid danger. They can even detect the body heat of creatures at night. So, they are able to strike out at prey in complete darkness! They also use their pits to find cool places to hide in hot weather.

Pit vipers have a well-developed sense of smell, too. A special sensor called the Jacobson's organ is located on the roof of the snake's mouth. This sensor helps the snake figure out what is in the area around it. A pit viper can then locate food, enemies, or other snakes.

A pit viper can be identified by the heat-sensing pit on each side of its head. However, if you can actually see this black-tailed rattlesnake's pits, you're too close!

DEFENSE

The pit viper's most common **predators** are birds of prey and some large mammals. The **nonvenomous** king snake also preys on pit vipers, primarily rattlesnakes. King snakes are not affected by the rattlesnake's venom.

Like most snakes, pit vipers usually hide when they feel threatened. But, rattlesnakes have another form of defense. The rattlesnake got its name from the "rattle" at the end of its tail. This consists of six to ten loosely connected segments of dried skin.

The rattlesnake shakes its tail as a warning to predators. This creates a buzzing sound. If this warning is ignored, the snake may bite. However, do not count on this noise to indicate that a rattlesnake is nearby. Some rattlesnakes don't shake their tail as a warning.

Most pit viper venom is **hemotoxic**. But, some rattlesnakes have **neurotoxic** venom. Pit viper bites are extremely serious and painful. **Hemotoxic venom** destroys the tissue and skin around the bite. However, the bites are usually not fatal because of **antivenin** treatment.

FOOD

Pit vipers usually eat warm-blooded prey, such as rodents. Occasionally they will eat frogs, fish, birds, and other snakes. Young pit vipers prey on lizards.

Most pit vipers are stealth hunters. They sit and wait coiled up until their next meal crosses their path.

Pit vipers use their heat-sensing pits to tell when a meal is near. Then, they **ambush** their prey.

When a pit viper strikes, its fangs rapidly swing forward and fill with **venom** as the mouth opens. The venom is then **injected** into the prey. The venom causes heavy bleeding inside the animal's body, and eventually heart failure.

The striking stance of a timber rattlesnake

This fer-de-lance is eating a whiptail lizard. The fer-de-lance is one of the largest species of pit vipers.

The heat-sensing pits help a pit viper locate its meal after the prey has been bitten. Like all snakes, pit vipers swallow their victims whole.

BABIES

Pit vipers living in **temperate** climates usually mate in the spring after they have emerged from hibernation. Males will travel great distances to mate. They often have to fight other males on the way.

During the summer, **pregnant** female rattlesnakes usually do not feed. Their young are born in the fall. However, pit vipers may not produce young every year.

Pit vipers are either **ovoviviparous** or viviparous. Ovoviviparous means the snakes hatch from eggs. Viviparous snakes develop inside of their mothers and are born live.

Most pit vipers are viviparous. Typically two to ten young snakes are born at a time. Copperheads are eight to ten inches (20 to 25 cm) long at birth. Rattlesnake babies typically can be six to eight inches (15 to 20 cm) long. Baby rattlesnakes are **venomous** at birth.

The bushmaster is one of the only species of pit viper that is **ovoviviparous**. The mother bushmaster lays 6 to 12 eggs. She remains with them until they hatch. The fer-de-lance has the most babies of all the pit vipers. It can produce litters of up to 86 snakes!

GLOSSARY

ambush - a surprise attack from a hidden position.

antivenin - a kind of medicine used to reverse the effects of a poisonous snakebite.

aquatic - growing or living in the water.

arboreal (ahr-BAWR-ee-uhl) - living in or frequenting trees.

family - a group that scientists use to classify similar plants or animals. It ranks above a genus and below an order.

habitat - a place where a living thing is naturally found.

hemotoxic - harmful to the circulatory system of the body.

hexagon - a flat figure that has six sides and six angles.

humid - having moisture or dampness in the air.

inject - to forcefully introduce a fluid into the body, usually with a needle or something sharp.

neurotoxic - harmful to the nervous system of the body.

ovoviviparous (OH-voh-veye-VIH-puh-ruhs) - a fish or reptile that carries its eggs inside it while they develop.

predator - an animal that kills and eats other animals.

pregnant - having one or more babies growing within the body.

temperate - having neither very hot nor very cold weather.

terrestrial (tuh-REHS-tree-uhl) - living on or in the ground.

thermoreceptor (thuhr-moh-rih-SEHP-tuhr) - a sensory organ that is stimulated by heat or cold.

venom - a poison produced by some animals and insects. It usually enters a victim through a bite or sting.

vertical - in the up-and-down position.

WEB SITES

To learn more about pit vipers, visit ABDO Publishing Company on the World Wide Web at **www.abdopub.com**. Web sites about these snakes are featured on our Book Links page. These links are routinely monitored and updated to provide the most current information available.

INDEX